THE JOY OF FLOWERS –
A COLORING BOOK OF CALM
AND SERENITY FOR ADULTS

BY:
GEN HAWTHORNE

THE JOY OF FLOWERS –
A COLORING BOOK OF CALM
AND SERENITY FOR ADULTS

Unwind from the daily grind and rediscover tranquility with this stress-free floral coloring book.

Immerse yourself in the delicate beauty of blossoming flora, each page meticulously designed to guide you on a journey of relaxation and creative expression.

Enjoy!

If you enjoy this coloring book, a great review on Amazon would be lovely.

All my best,

Gen Hawthorne.

Made in United States
Orlando, FL
30 June 2025